The

GW01270884

CITY OF DARKNESS

THE STORY OF JACKIE PULLINGER

Geoffrey Hanks

RMEP

RELIGIOUS AND MORAL EDUCATION PRESS

Religious and Moral Education Press
An imprint of Chansitor Publications Ltd
A Subsidiary Company of Hymns Ancient & Modern Ltd
St Mary's Works, St Mary's Plain
Norwich, Norfolk NR3 3BH

Chasing the Dragon, by Jackie Pullinger and Andrew Quicke (Hodder & Stoughton), is acknowledged as a primary reference source.

Photographs are reproduced by kind permission of Jackie Pullinger (pp. 4, 15, 22) and the South China Morning Post (pp. 3, 9, 11, 17). Cover photo courtesy of Jackie Pullinger.

First published 1984

New imprint 1991

Reprinted 1993

Printed in Great Britain by BPCC Wheatons Ltd, Exeter
ISBN 0 900274 44 1 *non net*

CITY OF DARKNESS

The Story of Jackie Pullinger

It was five o'clock in the morning when the telephone rang. Jackie Pullinger struggled out of bed and reached for the receiver.

"Hello," she muttered wearily.

"You've got to come quickly," a voice said. "There's been a break-in at the club. Everything's in a terrible mess."

Then the caller rang off, but Jackie had recognised the voice of Ah Ping, one of her youth club members.

She dressed quickly and hurried down into the street. Everyone else in Kowloon seemed to be still in bed. There were no buses about, so she ran as fast as she could. Soon she spotted a taxi, and asked the driver to take her to the Walled City. Within minutes she arrived at the club-room.

The damage was worse than she had feared. Benches, table-tennis bats and skateboards had been smashed and the bits thrown around the room. Books had been torn up, and sewage from the open drains in the street had been daubed all over the walls and the floor.

Jackie was so upset by what she saw that she wanted to sit down and cry. She had run the youth club for four years and believed the boys to be her friends. And now this had happened. Feeling angry and let down, she thought of giving up the work.

Then Jackie remembered how Jesus had also been betrayed by His friends. She spent the whole day cleaning up the mess, sobbing, getting ready to open the club again.

In the Walled City

In England, Jackie Pullinger had been a teacher. But she gave up teaching to become a missionary, because she felt that this was what God wanted her to do. Not knowing exactly where to go, she bought a ticket to Japan. When the ship reached Hong Kong, she decided to get off. She had no plans and knew no one in Hong Kong. All she had was about £6, her clothes and her guitar.

"God will show me what to do," she told herself, and waited to see what would happen.

Soon Jackie found a job at a mission school in the Walled City in Kowloon, part of Hong Kong. This is where it all started.

When Jackie first went there, the Walled City was a shanty town. Most people there lived in shacks made of wood, corrugated iron and other waste materials. A whole family often had to eat, sleep and even work in just one room.

The streets of the City were so narrow that hardly any light could get through to the houses, and as there was no electricity, the place was in almost total darkness. There were only four proper toilets in the whole area, and all the rubbish and sewage was thrown into the open drains.

There were said to be over 30 000 people living in the Walled City, an area the size of about six football pitches. In such a place, it was easy to hide. So it became a home for criminals, drug addicts, gamblers and gold smugglers. Anyone trying to escape from the police could find safety here. It was also the home of a large number of homeless boys, many of them thrown out by their parents.

Two views of the Walled City in the 1970s

As the police hardly ever entered the Walled City of Kowloon, it became a sort of no man's land, run by criminals, a centre for all that is worst in the world of crime and vice.

For many years, crime in the Walled City was controlled by two gangs of Triads. The original Triad Society was a group of men who worked secretly to overthrow the Manchus, who had conquered China in the seventeenth century. Today, however, Triads are mainly gangs of men and teenage boys who band together to make a lot of money by controlling crime.

When Jackie arrived in Hong Kong, the top man in the Walled City was a man called Goko. He was said to have several thousand followers. Each gang member promised to follow his "big brother" (the leader of the gang) and became his leader's "little brother", so all the gang members were part of the same family. The brothers were sworn to go to each other's aid if they were in trouble, even at the risk of death.

It was in this place that Jackie found work. Although she could not speak Chinese, she managed to teach the children singing and English! It was five years before she could speak Chinese well. Meanwhile, the children gave her a Chinese name: Poon Siu Jeh, or Miss Poon for short. (In China, the surname comes first, before the other names.)

On Saturday afternoons, Jackie ran a club for boys in the Walled City. They played football, table tennis and darts, and went roller-skating and boating. During the school holidays, Jackie took them camping, too. Later on, as the club became more popular, she opened it up on several evenings during the week as well.

A new beginning

Jackie's main aim was to get people in the Walled City to understand about Jesus, but, despite all her efforts, things did not go well. The youth club was not very successful and no one seemed to want to listen to her. She realised that she would have to put her message across in actions, not just in words.

Jackie began to give people practical help with their problems. She went with the boys to interviews for jobs or school places. If they were taken to court or sent to prison, she stood by them. She visited their homes to see what else she could do for them.

As the news of Jackie's work spread, all kinds of people in the City began to seek her help. They thought of her as a rich westerner and assumed she could get anything for them. Although Jackie could not meet many of their demands, she was prepared to be used like this. Anything, in fact, to show the love of Christ. But, as a missionary, she seemed to be a failure. No one would believe in Jesus.

Then she had an experience that completely changed her life and work. One day someone showed her that she was trying to do God's work in her own way, not in His way. She was not giving Him the chance to help her, even though she truly believed in Him. When Jackie realised this, she prayed and asked God to give her a new power, to fill her with His Spirit.

For a while nothing different happened. Jackie went on with her work in the Walled City in the same way as before. But then she found that she could pray to God in a new kind of language. It was not English, or any other language she could recognise. It was a kind of heavenly language, for prayer and worship. In the Bible, it is called "speaking in tongues". Jackie prayed in this new language and found that God began to do wonderful things for her. Without much effort on her part, people believed when she spoke to them about Jesus, drug addicts came off drugs and she had remarkable answers to prayers.

The evening after the break-in at the club, Jackie noticed a young man leaning in the doorway of the club.

"Got any trouble?" he asked.

"No, everything's fine," replied Jackie. "Why? Who are you anyway?"

"Goko sent me," he answered.

Jackie was taken aback. She had often sent messages to Goko, trying to arrange a meeting, but he had never bothered to reply. He was the top Triad gang leader in the City, too important to be bothered with a youth club organiser – and a woman, at that. But now he had sent one of his followers to guard the club.

"Goko said that if anyone bothers the club again, we'll deal with them." He mimed thrusting a dagger into a victim's belly.

"Thank you very much," said Jackie. "Would you please tell Goko that I am grateful, but I don't need his help. Jesus is looking after us."

"You must be crazy," he told her.

This was the first time Jackie met Winson. Night after night he returned to take up his post as youth club guard. He watched the boys at their games, enjoyed the hymn-singing and listened to the gospel talk Jackie gave every evening. But he always stayed just outside, in the street.

Later she discovered that Winson had run away from home as a boy and joined Goko's 14K Triad gang. Winson's gang number was 426. This meant he had a special rank: fight-fixer. His job was to arrange fights between rival gangs and choose the weapons. He was a very tough gang member. Jackie also found out that Winson was addicted to opium.

From time to time Jackie spoke to Winson and explained that Jesus could help him give up opium. He refused to believe. One night, however, when most of the boys had gone home, she invited him into the club. He accepted, and started to join in the hymn-singing. Jackie realised that he had been listening to her all the time he had been guarding the club. He had made up his mind to believe, and was prepared to give Jesus a try.

When he prayed with Jackie, Winson straight away began to speak to God in a wonderful language. As he prayed, he was completely cured of his drug addiction. He gave up opium without any pain or trouble.

"Now you must go and tell your gang that you believe in Jesus," Jackie told him. "Don't forget, no man can serve two Big Brothers. You can't follow Jesus and Goko."

Winson went back to his gang and told them what had happened to him. He also told Goko that he believed in Jesus. This was a brave thing to do, as he might have been beaten up. As it was, Goko decided to let him go.

A meeting with Goko

Goko had discovered who had messed up the club-room. He told the boys to return anything they had stolen and to go back to the club and behave.

"Can't go back," one of them told him. "We've broken up the place. She won't have us."

"Yes, she will," replied Goko. "Miss Poon is a Christian and she'll forgive you no matter how many times you offend."

At least, thought Jackie, Goko was beginning to understand the message she brought.

Some time later, Goko finally agreed to meet Jackie. He invited her to a restaurant and ordered food and drink. For a while, they said very little. Like two boxers, they were sizing each other up.

"Let's stop pretending," Jackie said at last. "You and I have nothing in common, so why are you being kind to me?"

"I believe you care about my followers like I do," Goko answered.

The youth club Jackie started in the Walled City

"Yes, I do, but I hate everything you stand for and I hate what you do."

"Poon Siu Jeh, you and I both have power," he went on. "But you have a power I don't have. I can't make my brothers quit drugs. I've watched you, and I believe your Jesus can. So I've decided to give the addicts to you."

"No. You only want them off drugs so they can fight for you. If they follow you they will certainly go back to the habit."

"All right, then. I'll give up my right to those who want to follow Jesus."

Jackie was amazed at this offer. The Triads never gave up their members. Membership was for life: once someone decided to join, there was no going back.

"I'll tell you what," Goko suggested as a final offer. "You can have all the rotten ones."

Jackie smiled. "All right. Those are the ones Jesus came for anyway."

The pact was agreed. Since then Jackie has helped many Triad members to become believers and give up drugs.

9

Drug addiction

For many years Hong Kong has been a centre for illegal drugs. In 1980 a Government report stated that there were an estimated 40 000 drug addicts in Hong Kong, most of them men. This amounted to about one per cent of the population. It is thought, however, that the true figure was nearer 100 000. Most of these drug-takers were addicted to either opium or heroin, powerful drugs prescribed as pain-killers for people suffering from severe illnesses.

People who misuse such drugs quickly become "hooked" and have great difficulty in giving up the habit, just as people can easily become addicted to alcohol or tobacco. It takes only fifteen days of continuous use of a drug like heroin to become hooked. Drug-taking is an expensive habit, too. Few addicts can afford to keep buying the drugs they need, so most of them turn to crime to get the money.

If an addict decides to give up drugs, he must be prepared to suffer terribly. The "withdrawal symptons" last for three days. During this time, the addict breaks out in a fever, begins to sweat, has terrible stomach cramps and is violently sick. He may attack people around him. Even if he pulls through, the cure is unlikely to last. Many addicts return to drugs immediately after their "cure".

Drugs offer addicts an escape from the hunger and poverty of the real world, but staying addicted to drugs is like signing your own death-warrant. An addict doesn't look after himself: he doesn't eat regular meals, or wash. He may become depressed and try to kill himself. Death often comes early for drug addicts.

The Hong Kong Government is very concerned about drug addiction. Since 1981 it has been spending over £20 million a year in its fight to stamp out the illegal drug trade. To help drug addicts, the Government has set up twenty treatment centres and there are two hospitals run by the

Society for the Aid and Rehabilitation of Drug Addicts. In addition, many prisoners in Hong Kong receive compulsory treatment every day they are in jail. But, as one report puts it, "Treatment centres will be around for many years, until young people can be educated to avoid this dangerous attraction."

Learning by mistakes

One man who has been able to help addicts in Hong Kong is Pastor Chan, a Christian minister. He has a farm outside Kowloon where drug addicts can stay if they want to break their drug habit. After withdrawal they stay on the farm for eighteen months, until they are completely healed and have grown stronger. These men are the only ex-junkies Jackie knew who had not gone back to drugs.

When Jackie tried to help drug addicts in the Walled City

Addicts in a Hong Kong opium den

she made some mistakes. Meeting Ah Tsoi made her see where she had gone wrong.

Ah Tsoi was only fifteen, but he looked like a living skeleton. His huge eye-sockets were dark, his face a yellowish grey. He had been addicted to drugs since the age of ten, when his stepfather had thrown him out of the house. He needed at least £1 a day to feed his habit, and got the money by robbing people. He had already been to prison for drug offences and was now on probation.

At first Jackie could not tell Ah Tsoi about Jesus because his mind was never clear enough for him to think straight. She waited, knowing there would be a time when she could get through to him. Each day she gave him a little money. Although she knew he would spend it on drugs, at least he would not be forced to mug and steal.

At last Jackie got Ah Tsoi a place on Pastor Chan's farm. She bought him new clothes and took him there, but he stayed only a few hours. He ran away because he could not stand the withdrawal pains. Jackie never saw him again.

When she heard that he had run away, Jackie was heartbroken. She lay on the floor and wept all day long. She had done everything she could for this boy, and had failed. She was not angry with God, but she could not understand why He had allowed it to happen.

The next day, as she walked about the Walled City, she noticed again the hundreds of drug addicts, openly smoking heroin. She prayed: "It would be worth my whole life if You could use me to help just one of them."

When Jackie met Pastor Chan, she spoke to him about her problem. He told her, "Miss Pullinger, you will make a very good worker because you care." Jackie realised that in a way she had cared too much about Ah Tsoi. She now understood that if an addict was to be freed from the habit he must want it for himself. Jackie could not save him.

Then she remembered what happened to Winson when he came to believe in Jesus. As he prayed in his new language he came off drugs without any pain or withdrawal symptoms. This was the answer. Jackie realised that in some wonderful way God was able to release addicts from drugs without suffering.

A good man

Ah Kei was a Triad gang leader and controlled a number of areas throughout Kowloon. He had hundreds of followers. After several attempts, Jackie finally persuaded him to meet her. The meeting was arranged for just after midnight.

"Poon Siu Jeh, if you can convert me, I'll give you a thousand disciples," he challenged.

"I can't convert you, Ah Kei," replied Jackie. "You can only believe it for yourself."

He invited Jackie to go with him on a tour of the shantytown where he controlled the gambling and drug dens.

"Poon Siu Jeh, do you look down on drug addicts?" he asked.

"No, I don't, because they are the people Jesus came into the world to save."

"Are you willing to be friends with one?" he went on.

"Some people in the Walled City criticise me because I am more willing to be friends with an addict than with those who think they are all right," she explained.

This seemed to satisfy Ah Kei.

Soon he stopped outside a tin hut. He led the way inside, to a brightly lit room where lots of people were playing various gambling games. They were startled to see a westerner. Ah Kei held up his hand for silence.

"Don't be afraid, she doesn't look down on us. She's a Christian."

Ah Kei invited Jackie to preach to the gamblers. They listened politely to what she had to say, then Jackie gave Bibles to anyone who was prepared to read one. The same thing happened in several other gambling dens that night.

In one of the dens, they brought a man who was doubled up with pain to see Jackie.

"Poon Siu Jeh, are you a doctor? Can you take him to a hospital?" they asked.

"No, I'm not a doctor, but I'll tell you what I can do – I'll pray for him."

Some of the men sniggered at this suggestion. But they showed her to a quiet room and brought the man in.

"I'll only pray on one condition – that nobody laughs. I'm going to pray to the living God," Jackie said firmly.

They agreed, and everybody stopped talking. Jackie laid her hands on the man's head and prayed in the name of Jesus that God would heal him. Immediately, his stomach relaxed and he got up, looking surprised. He was completely healed.

One of the men asked, "Is this the living God you've been telling us about?"

When Jackie left Ah Kei that night she gave him a Bible. In the weeks that followed, Jackie visited Ah Kei and read parts of the Bible to him. One night he told her that God had been speaking to him. She found this hard to believe, but it was true. He had been reading his Bible and was beginning to understand what Jesus was saying. He sat down with Jackie and prayed, asking God to take his life and make him a new person.

For the first time in many months, Ah Kei went home to his wife. He gave up his control over the gangs as well as all the money he got from his illegal activities. But he did not give up drugs completely, as Winson had done, and the problem troubled him for some time.

As his drug habit continued, Ah Kei began to lose hope.

Jackie and Ah Kei (second row, centre) at a baptism party

He felt he could not be saved. At last he gave up and decided to go back to the gangs. He planned a couple of robberies to get some money, but they failed. Once more he turned to Jackie for help.

Ah Kei told her that now he really wanted to come off drugs. In a last effort, he threw away his drugs and waited for the withdrawal pains to come. When they came, Jackie encouraged him to pray like Winson had done. Although healing did not come straight away, he prayed until the battle was won. In three days he was completely cured.

With his old life behind him, Ah Kei began to tell his relatives about Jesus. When they saw the change in him, many of them came to believe.

Ah Kei's father-in-law was so pleased about what had happened that he gave a special party to celebrate. "Once I was a young man, now I am old," he said, "but never before have I seen a bad man become a good man."

The Society of Stephen

When Winson gave up drugs, he continued to live in an opium den – he had no other home. It was the favourite meeting-place of his 14K brothers. So, although he had started a new life, he still came under the influence of the Triads. He was often tempted to go back to the gangs.

One day Jackie realised what a problem young believers like Winson were facing. If they were to remain free of drugs, they must be removed from dangerous temptations. They needed a home, like Pastor Chan's farm, where they could get away from the gangs.

Jackie decided to begin by opening her own home to some of these youngsters. First she would have to find a larger flat. A woman in the City offered her a flat, at a cheap rent. The walls were crumbling and there was a hole in the roof. There was no electricity and no lavatory, but Jackie saw it as an answer to her prayers.

She and another girl repaired and decorated the flat, and even managed to persuade some of the boys to help. Soon they moved in with their first four boys.

For a while Jackie again made the mistake of trying to do too much for them. As well as continuing with her usual work in the Walled City, she helped to care for the boys in the house. She cooked, fed and clothed them; she got them jobs or places at school. It was hard work. To make matters worse, the boys had never been brought up to live normally. They were used to being up all night and sleeping during the day. They got up when they woke up, did not eat at regular times and went to work only if they felt like it.

As more addicts became believers, somewhere else had to be found for them to live. Two of Jackie's friends, Ric and Jean Willians, were already helping with the work. They, too, decided to open their home to the boys. Then, with gifts of money, two further homes were bought.

16

In the first House of Stephen

Now Jackie was able to give the addicts support for twenty-four hours a day. The boys needed plenty of love and security, and time to adjust to a new way of living. When they left her, she wanted them to go as responsible members of society.

The next step was to form the houses into a society, with a legally registered name. This would be important when dealing with the courts or if there was trouble with the rent laws. They chose the name "Society of Stephen", sometimes shortened to S.O.S. The name was taken from a passage in the Bible about a man called Stephen, who spent his time helping needy people.

During the first four months, seventy-four boys passed through the homes. No boy was taken in who would not agree to stay at least ten days. But to give themselves a better chance of breaking completely free of their old habits of drug-taking, stealing and fighting, they really needed two years' care.

17

Most of the boys managed to settle down in their new home. They learned to do the jobs around the house, to go shopping and to care for the new arrivals. They had lessons in reading and English; they also read the Bible together and prayed.

The change in the boys was so marked that outsiders began to notice it. Most days the boys played football on a pitch next door to a government-run drug centre. The Stephen boys looked so fit that some of the addicts came and asked what their secret was.

Money

Strangely enough, money was never a serious problem during these times. Ever since Jackie stopped teaching, money to support her and her growing "family" had either arrived through the post or been given to her by people who knew her. Friends also gave her things like food and clothing.

"What do you do for money?" Jackie was once asked.

She hesitated, not wanting to sound bigheaded. "Oh, God looks after us. We pray for money and God sends it."

"O.K., but where does it come from?" the man went on.

At that moment there was a knock at the door. An old man walked in and handed Jackie an envelope addressed to "Jackie Pullinger, Walled City", nothing more. In it was an American hundred-dollar bill from someone she had never heard of. She showed her visitor the note. He smiled. "Enough, point taken," he said.

Some of the boys helped raise money for the homes by polishing floors. They had been given a floor-polishing machine and decided to go into the cleaning business. Tony, dressed in white trousers and plimsolls, was the foreman. He was good at organising and was able to get jobs waxing and cleaning floors. In this way, the boys not only helped to earn money but also took the chance to tell others about the gospel.

Going to court

The phone rang in Jackie's flat. It was Mau Jai.

"Johnny's been arrested. Please get to the police station quickly," he pleaded.

"How do you know?" asked Jackie.

"Can't talk here. Tell you later." Then the phone went dead.

By the time Jackie reached the police station, Johnny had already been charged. He had also signed a confession, admitting to a crime. It was obvious that he was not guilty, but Johnny realised that the police were out to get him. As he had a record, they would catch him sooner or later. He was ready to admit to the crime, if only to keep on good terms with the police.

Jackie pleaded with him to tell the truth, but he would not. She even spent a whole month's allowance to hire a lawyer to help him. When he got up in court, however, something made him tell the truth. Instead of being a short trial, it went on for over a week. But, in the end, the police won the case.

When the verdict was announced, the strain was too much for Jackie and she burst into tears. The inspector in charge of the case asked why she was crying.

"Because he didn't do it. He isn't guilty," she told him.

"Well, he's got a record as long as your arm. I wouldn't waste your time on him."

"That's not the point – he hasn't done this one."

"This is Hong Kong justice," the inspector replied. "Even if he hasn't done this one, he's done others. It's fair in the long run."

"That's not right," argued Jackie. "The name of Jesus stands for truth. We are called to tell the truth in court."

By now, other detectives had gathered round to listen. They just laughed at her, then went off together to celebrate their victory.

Johnny was sent to prison, but was shortly released. He returned to drugs, was arrested and sent back to prison. Jackie often went to visit him and he was always grateful to her for the way she stood up for him in court. But it was two years before he finally admitted that he needed to accept the gospel. He became a believer and came off drugs. Later he got a job as a nurse – on a ward for drug addicts.

Leaving court one day Jackie heard a shout behind her. She turned to see a boy being led into the dock. He was waving wildly at her, trying to attract her attention.

"Poon Siu Jeh, I've been framed – help me," he cried.

Without knowing whether he was telling the truth, Jackie went to the magistrate.

"Your Honour, I am not familiar with the accused, but I think it possible that he does not have legal aid. Could you remand the case, so that enquiries could be made?"

Although this was unusual, the magistrate agreed. When she met the boy in his cell, she was given only two minutes to speak to him.

"Listen to me," said Jackie. "I have no time to tell you about Jesus. But if you call on His name, He will hear you. He is God."

When Jackie met him again the next day, the boy's face was clear and happy. He told her that his name was Sorchuen. He had prayed to Jesus for help and now felt quite different. However, he was found guilty and sent to prison. By now Jackie was sure he had not committed the crime. Once again she hired a lawyer and set about finding evidence to prove the case. A new trial was arranged.

The police inspector was annoyed because Jackie was taking all this trouble over what he said was "a no-good boy".

"Why waste time on a boy like this?" he asked.

"Because I believe he is innocent."

"But he has more than a dozen crimes to his name," he told Jackie.

"Yes, I know, but he did not commit this particular crime."

At the end of the trial, Sorchuen was found "not guilty" and set free. Sorchuen was just one of several people Jackie has been able to help in this way. But she always insists that they tell the truth.

Refugees

By 1979 the drug problem in the Walled City had become less serious and Jackie started to spend a great deal of her time working at a refugee camp, looking after some of the thousands of people who have fled to Hong Kong.

Since the end of the Second World War, millions of people in the Middle East and Asia have lost their homes or been driven from their country by wars, or because of arguments between governments or political parties. In 1949 the first wave of refugees arrived in Hong Kong from China after Communist forces took over the Chinese Government. When the Vietnam War ended in 1975, Vietnamese refugees also began flooding into Hong Kong. The population of Hong Kong shot up from 600 000 to over 5 million.

One of the biggest problems the Hong Kong Government faced was how to house all these people. Some of the refugees have been found homes in other countries, but many of them are still living there in large camps. They wait and hope that one day someone will offer them a home.

A group of orphaned Vietnamese refugees on an outing with Jackie and friends, 1980

The camp where Jackie worked is at Tuen Mun, a few kilometres outside Kowloon. It used to be a factory, but in 1982 housed 1700 Vietnamese refugees. They sleep 200 to 250 in a room, with just enough space for each person to spread a sleeping-mat on the floor.

One of Jackie's jobs was to assist a missionary doctor called Donald Dale, who opened a clinic at the camp. She also held daily classes for refugees who wanted to learn English, and ran a weekly meeting for Bible teaching.

Some of the refugees in the camp came to believe in Jesus. This started before they reached Hong Kong. As they escaped by boat, they ran into many kinds of problems. And as people often do when in trouble, they prayed to God – and had answers to their prayers.

When refugees on one boat ran out of food and water, they prayed. Soon a passing ship stopped and gave them new supplies. Another group prayed and a helicopter flew over and dropped them some food. When they reached Hong Kong, these people were only too ready to learn about the God who had saved them.

The camp chairman was one of those who became a believer. He had been arrested in Vietnam for trying to leave the country. In prison, he shared a cell with a Christian pastor, who explained the gospel to him. He expected to be put to death, but was instead set free. He finally escaped to Hong Kong. The boat he was in broke down and began to drift. He prayed to God; another boat sighted them and towed them to safety. It was this incident that made him believe.

In the early 1980s the drug problem in the Walled City began to get worse and Jackie has once again been spending a lot of time helping gang members and drug addicts. Many of the Triads have come to ask for her help.

In 1983, however, something remarkable happened: Goko, the leader of the 14K Triad, became a Christian. He was baptised and took the Christian name "New Paul".

Many of Jackie's former drug addicts have fully recovered and have begun to live useful lives again. One of the boys from the Society of Stephen probably spoke for all of them when he said, "I am happy for the first time in my life, and for the first time in my life I can smile."

BIOGRAPHICAL NOTES

Jackie Pullinger was born in Croydon, South London, in 1944. After leaving school, she went to the Royal College of Music to study the piano and the oboe. She gained her A.R.C.M. diploma and a degree in music. Whilst at college, she became a Christian and began to think about becoming a missionary. Her attention became focused on Hong Kong, but efforts to find a teaching post there failed. She finally took "a slow boat to China" and arrived in Hong Kong in November 1966.

The youth club in the Walled City was opened in July 1967, and the first House of Stephen was set up in 1972. Several more followed. Two television films about her work were shown in 1976 and 1978, and Jackie's book, *Chasing the Dragon*, was published in 1980. She has been invited to Holland, Germany, Singapore and Japan to preach in prisons and churches.

THINGS TO DO

A Test yourself

Here are some short questions. See if you can remember the answers from what you have read. Then write them down in a few words.

1 What job did Jackie find in the Walled City?
2 Name at least two of the Saturday-afternoon activities she arranged for the youth club.
3 What was Jackie's main aim in the Walled City?
4 Why did Goko send Winson to the youth club?
5 Which gang members did Goko agree to let Jackie have?
6 What has the Hong Kong Government done to help drug addicts?
7 Why do drug addicts go to Pastor Chan's farm?
8 How many boys passed through the Society of Stephen's homes in the first four months?
9 Where did Jackie get the money she needed to look after her growing "family"?
10 From which two countries have the refugees in Hong Kong escaped?

B Think through

These questions need longer answers. Think about them, and then try to write two or three sentences in answer to each one. You may look up the story again to help you.

1 Write a description of living conditions in the Walled City.
2 Why do you think so many criminals made their home there?
3 What is a Triad gang? How do the members look after one another?
4 What happens to addicts who stop taking drugs and try to break the habit?
5 Did becoming a Christian change Ah Kei's life? In what ways?
6 How does the Society of Stephen help drug addicts? What success does it have?
7 Why have thousands of refugees come to Hong Kong? Describe the work Jackie did in the refugee camps.

C Talk about

Here are some questions for you to discuss together. Try to give reasons for what you say or think. Try to find out all the different opinions which people have about each question.

1 Jackie tried to follow the teaching of Jesus by "loving her neighbour" and "walking the second mile". What do you think these phrases mean? Was Jackie too soft-hearted?

2 Why do you think some people misuse drugs? What are the dangers of this habit? Can cigarettes and alcohol cause similar problems?

3 Why did Jackie insist that those she helped in court should tell the truth? Is it best to tell the truth, even if it means being found out and punished?

D Find out

Choose one or two of the subjects below and find out all you can about them. History books, geography books and newspapers may be useful. You could also use reference books in your school or public library to look up some of the names and places.

1 *Hong Kong*

(a) Find out how and when Hong Kong became a British colony. What important event is due to take place there in 1997?

(b) Which races of people live in Hong Kong? What are their religious beliefs and what languages do they speak? What kinds of work do they do?

(c) Look at some pictures of Hong Kong. How has the Government overcome the problem of lack of flat land for housing and industry?

(d) Why has Hong Kong become an important port and air-traffic centre? Find out how the railway system is being improved.

(Read *Fact Sheet: Hong Kong* and *An Introduction to Hong Kong*, available from the Hong Kong Government Office – see p.29.)

2 *Refugees*
   (a) For what reasons are people forced to leave their country as refugees and settle elsewhere? Write a short account of refugees in the past or in the present from any part of the world.

   (b) Draw a map of South-East Asia, marking on it Hong Kong, China, Laos, Vietnam, Cambodia and their main cities.

   (c) Find out what one of the following does to help refugees: Christian Aid, Oxfam, the TEAR Fund and the Save the Children Fund (see p.29).

   (d) Find out either about refugees who have come to live in Britain, or how refugees are helped in Hong Kong. (Read *The Boat Refugees from Vietnam* and *Vietnamese Refugees*, available from the British Refugee Council, and other leaflets available from the U.N. High Commissioner for Refugees – see p.29.)

3 *Drugs*
   (a) Find out about drugs that can be used to ease pain and cure illnesses. Why should drugs be prescribed only by a doctor?

   (b) Drug addicts take drugs illegally, with terrible results. Find out about some of the drugs misused in this way and about the effects they have.

   (c) Read about some of the addicts in Jackie Pullinger's book *Chasing the Dragon* (see p.29). How did their faith in Jesus help them to overcome their addiction?

   (d) Smoking and drinking are accepted by many people simply as enjoyable habits, but tobacco and alcohol are drugs that can be very harmful. Write an account of the ways in which they can damage the human body.

4 *Speaking in tongues*
   (a) Acts 2 in the Bible describes how the first Christians received the gift of tongues from the Holy Spirit at Pentecost. Read this chapter and try to describe what happened.

(b) Chapter 5 of Jackie Pullinger's book *Chasing the Dragon* tells how she began to speak in tongues. How did this affect her work as a missionary? Find out how the gift of tongues affected some of the drug addicts she worked with.

(c) Read what Saint Paul says about the gifts of the Holy Spirit in 1 Corinthians 12: 1-12 and 27-31 and 1 Corinthians 14. How important does he think the gift of tongues is and how does he suggest it should be used?

(d) Other people have written about receiving the gift of tongues. For example, Lieutenant-Colonel Merlin Carrothers, an army chaplain in Vietnam, tells his story in *Prison to Praise* (see p.30). Write a short account of how this gift affected him and some of his fellow soldiers who believed in Jesus.

USEFUL INFORMATION

Addresses

Hong Kong Government Office
6 Grafton Street
London W1X 3LB.

United Nations High
    Commission for Refugees
36 Westminster Palace Gardens
Artillery Row
London SW1 1RR.

British Refugee Council
Bondway House
3/9 Bondway
London SW8 1SJ.

The Save the Children Fund
157 Clapham Road
London SW9.

Oxfam
274 Banbury Road
Oxford OX2 7DZ.

Christian Aid
240/250 Ferndale Road
London SW9 8BH.

TEAR Fund
11 Station Road
Teddington
Middlesex TW11 9AA.

Teachers' Advisory Council
    on Drug Education
2 Mount Street
Manchester M2 5NG.

The Health Education Council
78 New Oxford Street
London WC1A 1AH.

N.B. It is best if only one person in each class writes off for information. Remember to enclose a stamped, addressed envelope for the reply. In most cases, a postal order for at least 50p would also be helpful, if you want plenty of material.

More books to read
Alcohol and Tobacco and *Drug Takers*, by John L. Foster (Edward Arnold, Checkpoint series) (P).
Chasing the Dragon, by Jackie Pullinger and Andrew Quicke (Hodder & Stoughton) (T).
Drugs, by W.J. Hanson (Longman, Enquiries series) (P).

Friend of Drug Addicts, by R.J. Owen (R.M.E.P.) (P).
Prison to Praise, by Merlin Carrothers (Hodder & Stoughton) (T).
Vietnamese in Britain, by Penny Mares (Health Education Council) (T).

A variety of leaflets and other material relating to refugee problems is also available from Christian Aid, the British Refugee Council, the Save the Children Fund, the TEAR Fund and Oxfam.

(T) = suitable for teachers and older pupils
(P) = suitable for younger pupils

Films

Attacking the Dragon and *Hong Kong Style*, from the Hong Kong Government Office.

The Cross and the Switchblade (115 min), colour. A film about David Wilkerson's work among drug addicts in New York. Unsuitable for children under fourteen. Also available on video. Available from National Film Crusade, P.O. Box 100, Westbury on Trym, Bristol BS9 4QH.

I Am a Refugee (34 min), *Only When It Rains* (11 min) and *Road to Survival* (40 min), all colour. From the U.N. High Commission for Refugees or from Concord Films Council, 201 Felixstowe Road, Ipswich, Suffolk IP3 9BJ.

Filmstrips

Images of Indo-China and *Refugees*, from Christian Aid.

Slides

Gale in Hospital and *Hong Kong: A Crowded Environment*, from The Slide Centre, 143 Chatham Road, London SW11 6SR.